How the F*ck Do You Get into Medical School?

A Candid Guide for Applying to Medical School

By: James West

Copyright © 2020 by James West
All rights reserved. This book or any portion thereof
may not be reproduced or used in any manner whatsoever
without the express written permission of the publisher
except for the use of brief quotations in a book review.

Printed in the United States of America

Table of Contents

Table of Contents   3
Dedication   5
Introduction   7
Pre-Application   11
  Deciding to be a Doctor   13
    Time commitment   13
    Financial   15
    Lifestyle   17
    Family   18
      Having a family during medical school   18
      Having a family during residency   19
      Time for family and friends during medical school and residency   20
    Depression and suicide in the medical profession   20
    Personal Satisfaction   20
  School   22
    High School   22
    Undergraduate   22
    Graduate School   24
  Extracurricular   25
  Awards   26
  MCAT   27
Applying to Medical School   29

Which medical schools to apply?	31
Letter of Intent	32
Reference Letters	33
Extracurricular activities	34
Interviews	34
CanMEDS	36
MMI	36
Results	39
What do I do now that I got into medical school?	41
What do I do if I don't get into medical school?	42
Try again	42
Medical School Abroad	45
US MD Schools	45
US DO Schools	46
Caribbean Medical Schools	46
Australian Medical Schools	46
European Medical Schools	46
Switch to an alternative career	47
Graduate school	47
Conclusion	49
Resources	53

Dedication

This book is dedicated to the many medical school applicants for their dedication in pursuing a profession devoted to healing and helping our fellow mankind.

Introduction

The information is provided in an honest and helpful manner to guide the reader through every stage of the application process. Advice that candidates wished they had known early on is helpful. There are many areas regarding applying to Medicine that are discussed and generally not often talked about or are often nebulous to most candidates. This book is designed to give insight, clarity and strategy in applying to medical school. Due to increasing competitiveness of applying to medical school, many applicants often require multiple rounds of application. Consequently, this book addresses areas of troubleshooting in the application process to minimize the mistakes and number of trial and error so the candidate can be successful in applying to medical school as quickly as possible.

Thank you for reading this book and I wish you luck on your journey into Medicine!

Pre-Application

Deciding to be a Doctor

Should you apply to be a doctor?

Applying to be a doctor can be a conundrum because the application process is competitive. The earlier you prepare the better the chances. But you need to know early enough that you want to be a doctor. Committing to be a doctor also means committing about a decade of your life to train to be a doctor. The decision to apply to be a doctor is a significant decision point in one's life. The first question before applying is to be clear if you actually want to be a doctor. Answering this critical question requires understanding what it means to be a doctor and what is it like to train to be a doctor. Understanding the answers to these questions enables you to know what you're really getting yourself into. Answers to these questions have different levels of understanding and complexity that we will address sequentially.

Time commitment

The preparation and commitment begin in university in selecting the courses required to apply to medical school. Prior to applying, most people spend a year or dedicate a summer to study for the Medical College Admission Test (MCAT), which is the exam required to apply to medical school. The application process will take approximately a year. This can be a significant time commitment if someone changes their mind to not be a physician. Changing the decision to apply to medical school could mean several years lost, courses taken unnecessarily, and unnecessary studying for the MCAT. People have needed to undergo several additional years of post-secondary education because they changed their decision to be a physician near the end of their undergraduate degree. However, changing the decision to be a physician even just prior to starting medical school can be the better answer for people who realize that being a physician is not the correct decision for them. The courses taken during medical school cannot be transferred to another degree or program. The financial expenses of medical school are high.

Once you're accepted in medical school, you have committed to at least four years of medical school followed by a residency program lasting between 2 to 5 years. Depending on the specialty training, many will also be followed by a fellowship that lasts 1 to 2 years. In total, that is at least 6 years and can be 11 years of training after you get into medical school. People can get into medical school after 2 years of university in a few places. Many get in after 3-4 years of undergraduate education. Some applicants have completed a master's degree or PhD which can be 2 to 5 years in length. The total educational time commitment after high school can vary from 8 to 20 years. Most spend approximately 14 years of postsecondary education. Furthermore, most people are undergoing this training process during their 20's to 30's. One can argue that the second to third decades of life can be the prime of your life. The decision to commit to this long process deserves careful consideration. But there are other considerations that we will continue to discuss.

Financial

The financial burden begins with the student debt accumulated from the undergraduate degree. The debt further accumulates during graduate studies in some applicants. This can be in the range of $100,000 depending on the type of degree, number of degrees and financial support. For many applicants, student loans make up the bulk of the financial burden at this stage. Each application to a medical school costs approximately $100. Many applicants apply to multiple medical schools. The cost of the plane ticket and accommodation for each medical school interview can be in the range of several hundred dollars. The cost of medical school applications and interviews can be significant depending on the number of schools. The total cost of medical school applications and interviews can be in the range several thousand dollars per application cycle. Some applicants require multiple application cycles.

Medical school expenses include tuition, textbooks, equipment and living expenses. The medical school expenses vary depending on the school and location. On average, these medical school expenses is approximately $250,000 over four years. Many of the major banks will provide $150,000 to $275,000 of low interest loans for medical school. Banks often only require interest-only payments while in school. Government student loans can also assist with the financial needs. The cost for applying to residency in the final year of medical school can be significant. Many medical students apply to multiple schools or programs. The residency interviews are in different cities. Each interview away from the home school requires a plane ticket and accommodation. The cost of applying to residency can be several thousands of dollars. The final year medical student often has already accumulated significant debt. The cost of apply to residency can lead to difficult financial situations, especially if they forget to budget for this expense.

Salaries during residency range from approximately $45,000 to $75,000. The salary during residency varies between universities. The salary during residency gradually increase with each year of residency. Major banks are often willing to increase the line of credit limit during residency. Government student loans can play a role in residency. The amount loaned from government student loans is often mitigated by the income earned during residency. Furthermore, some residents may have reached the lifetime limit allowable for government student loans. There are many significant expenses during residency including attending review courses, examination fees, flights and accommodations to fellowship interviews. Conferences and review courses are often in various cities with associated flight and accommodation costs. In total, these costs on average are approximately $50,000. There are many expected large expenses during medical school and residency. These large expenses are not often talked about. Many may not realize even deep into medical school or residency. Financial planning and budgeting are important during medical training. The financial burden during training along with the frugal lifestyle for nearly a decade of training is a factor to consider.

By the end of residency, that person is still carrying the debt from undergraduate, medical school, and residency. The total debt at the end of residency can often be in the range of $300,000. At the end of training, the typical person is in their early 30's with a debt that is equivalent to a mortgage. Many of their peers have been working for a decade. Their peers have often advanced into senior positions in their profession with commensurate salaries and partially paid off mortgage. The salary of a physician varies between specialties and location. The salary for physicians on average is approximately $250,000. The salary figure gross income and doesn't include expenses to operate a clinic or taxes. The working physician will be able to pay off their debt within a few years. The physician will catch up with their peers and eventually outpace their peers financially but with the sacrifices made early on.

Lifestyle

Committing to be a physician is both a career and lifestyle choice. Many people may not realize or underestimate the physician career's impact on their lifestyle during training and in practice.

The lifestyle of an undergraduate student applying for medical school is essentially the same as a typical undergraduate but with the added effort that we will discuss. First, the courses for the prerequisites to apply for medical school are science base. Many science courses will have labs which result in more time spent at school. The prerequisite courses typically be earlier morning classes and require more memorization compared to courses in other disciplines. Second, the applicant will need to spend at least a summer dedicated to studying for the MCAT. This is a summer of fun or work enjoyed by many of your peers. Third, the applicant will need to prepare for medical school interviews while studying for senior level courses. Finally, the extracurricular activities need to be balanced with the university and medical school application process. Extracurricular activities are discussed in the respective section.

During the first two years of medical school, the typical medical student will be in the classroom approximately 8 hours a day. They self-study in their own time after lectures. The last two years of medical school involves being at the hospital 8 hours a day. They are required to be on-call 24 hours every few days depending on the rotation. During the clinical rotations, medical student's self-study on their own time as well. This will continue into residency for another 2 to 5 years depending on the specialty. The practicing physician may continue this schedule or have more or less call duty depending on the specialty.

Family

Having a family during medical school

Having a child while in medical school is difficult for both a mother and father. The time schedule, time on call, and need to study outside of working hours increases the difficulty for being a parent training in medicine. It is possible but it is a difficult. Preparation and organization are essential if you are planning to have children during medical school. Children are financially and physically taxing. The lack of income during medical school increases the difficulty. Enlisting people or family to help with raising a child can be very beneficial.

Having a family during residency

Having a child during residency is easier financially because residents get a salary. The income allows for hiring a nanny, babysitter, or paying for child care. The challenge of studying outside of work persists. Balancing a busy work schedule is more difficult while studying for the graduation exams. Planning and organization with help raising the child is prudent if planning to raise a child during residency.

Taking time off during medical school or residency to have a child is an option. More time to raise a child is traded for delay in graduation. Period of lower income during residency coincides during a period of increased spending in raising a child. It is a balance of valuing the prioritizing of starting a family early versus completion of a long period of medical training with its associated challenges. The decision is difficult for both men and women. Women may face a higher time pressure when placed in a situation weighing the biological clock of increased complications of having children at an older age. The pressure is exacerbated by learning about the complications during medical school and residency.

Time for family and friends during medical school and residency

Due to the nature of the long work schedule and being on call, it can be difficult to balance a healthy relationship outside of school and work. Being on call results in people being available during inhospitable hours. Consequently, there may be periods of times when medical students or residents are not available to spend time with friends and family during regular hours. Family and friends need to be patient and understanding. It can be particularly taxing for medical trainees during exam periods. Maintaining healthy relationships and friendship is important. Social networks help medical trainees be more resilient to the stresses of their medical training. Effort is required from both the learner and their friends and family.

Depression and suicide in the medical profession

We have talked about the work schedule, being on call, pressures at work and in school. Combined with the personalities that are drawn into the medical profession, it creates the perfect situation to breed depression and suicide. Consequently, the medical profession does have a higher than average rate of depression, suicide and burnout. Approximately one in five people in the medical profession experience depression, suicide or burnout.

Personal Satisfaction

We have talked a lot about negatives of training and being a medical professional. It is important to be aware of these factors in order to make an informed decision. Information on these topics is often difficult to find. There are benefits of being in a medical profession. It can be worthwhile for some people after weighing the negative aspects. The primary draw to the medical profession is the personal satisfaction of a rewarding career with a direct positive impact in people's daily lives. The patient interaction can be satisfying at times. But like any personal interaction, rewarding moments exist with times of conflict and frustration. There is relative work security and good remuneration in the healthcare profession. Many of these qualities exist in careers that have a shorter duration of training. Prior to selecting the medical training route, people should explore other careers and professions.

Short of going through the medical training process and practicing, there are many ways for people better understand the life of a physician. Interested individuals may talk to different physicians. Talk to people who work with physicians such as the nurses, support staff, and physician's family members to get different perspectives. Shadowing physicians in their various work settings. Volunteer in different health care settings including the hospital, clinic, and senior centers.

The effort of understanding the pros and cons of being a physician will inform your decision to be a doctor. You will thank yourself for making the correct career and lifestyle choice. The informed decision will be useful in the application process. Medical schools want to ensure they are selecting the appropriate candidate who understands being a physician. Understanding the pros and cons of being a physician helps show the medical school that the applicant will commit to the training and be happy with their career choice.

School

High School

The grades, courses, and extracurricular activities in high school generally has a relatively low impact on the application. Their role is mainly to get you into university. It is also important to develop the skills to succeed academically in university. People who did not do well in high school can be relieved that it doesn't have a direct impact on your application. However, they may need to work harder in university. People who do well high school can't rest on their laurels because university results will be the primary focus of the medical school application. Avoiding burnout in high school is important. Especially in people who have decided early in life that they want to be a doctor. Burnout prevention is important for applicants with parental pressure. The applicant and parents both need to understand the importance of avoiding burnout.

Undergraduate

The marks, courses, and extracurricular activities during the undergraduate degree provides the bulk of the weighting for the medical school application. The prerequisite courses are mostly in science. Slight variations between schools exist.

Comparing entrance requirements from different schools to ensure applicants meet all the requirements for the different schools is important. Taking a full course load is preferable because it is evidence of the applicant's ability to manage the course load in medical school. Taking only a few courses as a part time student to try to get high marks may not be the best strategy. Medical schools may question ability to handle the course load in medical school. Medical schools may inquire for the reason for extended periods when the applicant has been a part time student. The grades from the prerequisite courses, average grade per year, and overall marks from all courses are considered in the application process. Some people may try to complete courses that they have an aptitude. Leveraging an ability to get high marks outside of the prerequisite courses to increase the average of the overall mark is a strategy. Completing degrees in disciplines to obtain a higher mark does not guarantee entry into medical school. There may be limited options if the applicant completes degree with low prospects of employment or interest in continuing with graduate studies.

Pursuing a degree in an allied health care profession or other professional degree may provide a safety net of a career if the applicant does not get into medical school. These degrees may contain courses that are more subjective or difficult to get high marks. For example, clinical rotations in professions such as pharmacy or nursing can be more subjective in grading. Subjectivity in evaluation introduces uncertainty in grade optimization for medical school admission. The uncertainty is balanced with the benefit of a career regardless of medical school admission results. This is a personal decision based on the individual risk adversity, personal strengths and weaknesses.

Many people are concerned about the average mark required for medical school admission. A level of academic ability is desired for medical school admission to complete the academic nature of the studying. After a threshold, higher marks may not be as important as demonstrating the other attributes that medical schools are searching for in their candidates. Deficiency in these other attributes can impair a candidate from getting into medical school despite a perfect GPA. We will go over these other attributes in more detail in the extracurricular and interview section. Generally, an average mark greater than 70% is necessary. Grades above 80% is competitive. Striving for marks much higher than 80% at the expense of your ability to demonstrate the other desirable attributes medical schools want in their candidates as a physician could be detrimental to the overall application. Most of these other attributes are demonstrated in the extracurricular activities.

Graduate School

There is an increasing number of applicants with graduate degrees as medical school admissions become more competitive. Many medical school applicants attend graduate school after unsuccessful medical school applications. Their goal is to increase the chances of getting into medical school. Graduate school can be helpful in the medical school application. Graduate school is further discussed in the graduate school section on "What if you don't get into medical school?" chapter.

Extracurricular

After reaching a threshold for your grades, the candidates are differentiated based on their extracurricular activities. The extracurricular activities are important. Insufficient extracurricular activities can be a reason many applicants with very high grades don't get into medical school. Focusing on getting high grades with minimal extracurricular activity is a common reason for applicants not getting into medical school. Some applicants with high grades will take a year after they graduate to expand their extracurricular activity and are successful in getting into medical school.

Select extracurricular activities that highlight certain characteristics and experiences that medical schools value in their candidates. You want to have extracurricular activities that demonstrate your exposure to Medicine and understand what it entails to choose to be a physician. This can include volunteering at the hospital or medical community outreach programs. Extracurricular activities that demonstrate your leadership ability such as holding an executive position in a club or local organization. Leadership can be demonstrated by organizing an event or fundraiser in your community. Combining activities such as organizing a fundraiser for a medically related project allows you to be efficient by killing two birds with one stone. Traveling to different countries allows you demonstrate your maturity, life experience, and exposure to diversity. Traveling also provides interesting stories that you can share in the interview. Traveling to different countries to perform and organize humanitarian efforts in a medically related project allows you to combine several attributes in a single activity.

Remember to outline the different aspects and attributes that the medical school wants to hear that can occur in a single activity.

Volunteering for projects generally demonstrates altruism which is looked upon favorably by medical schools. Volunteer projects also generally allows you to be involved in more projects with varying responsibilities than in a job. Volunteering may involve being in leadership positions which you can use to expand your abilities. Working and getting paid for various jobs can be used to demonstrate many of the attributes but is often considered in a separate section of the application under employment. The application is often geared towards demonstrating some degree of volunteering.

Awards

There is usually a section for your awards and accomplishments. Include awards and accomplishments from school, work or extracurricular activities. Most people will generally only need a few items in this section. There are only a few applicants with truly outstanding accomplishments. You don't need to excessively worry about the magnitude of your accomplishments. There are medical school applicants with amazing accomplishments or awards. But most of the people that get into medical school don't have these extraordinary accomplishments. Furthermore, some people with extraordinary accomplishments still don't get into medical school because the other aspects of the application are not strong enough to meet the threshold.

MCAT

The Medical College Admission Test (MCAT) is a test that most schools require for their applications. Some people study for the exam on their own without courses. Most people take an exam preparation course which includes all the study preparation material, practice exams, lectures and will guide you along the study process to ensure you stay on track. The courses are relatively expensive and costs around $1,000 to $2,000. Some courses run throughout the school year on evenings and/or weekends. There are courses that run during the summer that require most of your time to study during the summer. The different sections of the MCAT tests different aspects ranging from reading and comprehension to basic science knowledge. You want to score at least 10 out of 15 in each section. Scoring sufficiently well in all sections is important. Scoring exceptionally well in some sections but not meeting the minimum requirement in other sections can be enough to not be admitted. For example, candidates can score 13 to 15 in a few sections and have one section below 10. The one section scoring low significantly decreases the strength of the application. It is more important to have each section meeting the threshold than score high in some sections with some sections not meeting the threshold.

> *"To cut down a tree in five minutes, spend three minutes sharpening your axe."*
> *Abraham Lincoln*

Applying to Medical School

At the stage of filling out the application to medical schools, you have decided to apply to Medicine, met the course requirements and written the MCAT.

Which medical schools to apply?

Applying to medical school is a competitive process. You want to optimize your chances of getting into medical school. The more schools you apply, the greater the chance of you getting in. You want to apply to as many schools as you can. Apply to all the Canadian schools if possible. However, there are certain in province requirements for each province. There is usually a limited number of seats for out of province applicants for each province. Approximately 10% of the seats are for out of province applicants. Each province has different criteria to be considered an in-province applicant. It is advised to review the criteria for each province. If you can meet the criteria for another province, this raises your chances of getting into a Canadian medical school significantly. For example, some provinces would consider you are an in-province applicant after living for a certain period of time prior to applying. If you are doing your undergraduate degree in a different province you may be considered an in-province applicant in the province you are attending the university. Some provinces consider applicants as in-province if you are born in that province. Some medical schools consider applicants as in province if they have lived in a certain province for a certain period. Some provinces do not favor in or out of province and treat everyone equally.

You can increase your chances of getting into medical school if you are willing to consider medical schools in the

United States. Applying to medical schools abroad is discussed in more detail in the "Medical schools abroad" section under the "What if I don't get into medical school?" chapter.

The limiting factor for applying to multiple medical schools include cost, time, and interest. It can be quite costly to apply to multiple schools with each application fee costing on average $100. There are over a hundred schools in the US. The deadlines for each school and timeline for application can vary slightly. You want to be aware of the deadlines prior to applying. There can be a lot of effort in writing customized letters of intent for each school. Filling out individual forms for each school can be time consuming. Although, significant portions of the letter can be re-used in most of the schools. The application effort is mitigated by a centralized application process where forms are sent to all the schools in the US. There might be a few custom parts of the application to add for each school in addition to the general form for applying to US schools. Similarly, some provinces in Canada such as in Ontario also has a centralized application form.

Letter of Intent

The letter of intent can vary slightly in the topic between the schools. Follow the prompt for the letter for each school. Generally, the letter of intent describes the reason you are applying to medical school. You want to demonstrate that you understand what it means to be a physician. Demonstrate what you've done to prove you understand the meaning of being a physician. Incorporate as many relevant life experiences as possible. If you have experiences and qualifications such as graduate work, you can incorporate that into the letter as well. The introspective exploration of the reasons you want to be a physician is the mental work for the letter of intent. The work we put in at the beginning in understanding being a physician will help with writing the letter of intent. The extracurricular work provides the foundation to build your letter. Remember to proofread your letter and get input from other people if possible. There is often a proofreading service in the university to proofread and obtain input on your letter. Sometimes an English major friend can be helpful in this regard. Try to be clear, concise and organized with your letter.

Customize each letter to each school. The bulk of the letter can often be reused because all medical schools generally want to know your reason for being a doctor. Your rationale to be a physician is likely the same for each school. However, your reason for applying for each school should be tailored to the school.

Reference Letters

Reference letters include an academic reference letter from a professor from a course or research work. Personal reference letter can be from volunteering, community service or work. Choose the people who can write the best reference for you. But also choose references that give you the most diverse perspective. In general, the key is to avoid having a poor reference letter. Most candidates will have positive reference letters. After a while, the reference letters all sound the same. Generally, reference letters for most applicants are similarly positive with only a few exceptional reference letters.

Extracurricular activities

The extracurricular component of the application should be filled with as many extracurricular activities as possible. The quality and quantity of extracurricular activities are assessed. You want a few high-quality extracurricular activities. High-quality extracurricular activities demonstrate your leadership skills, interest in Medicine, maturity, and volunteerism. Then you want to maximize the quantity and breadth of extracurricular and volunteer activities. These other extracurricular activities can vary in depth and time but often offers interesting experiences. Remember to outline the major qualities in each of the extracurricular activities even though it is a single activity. Outlining the various qualities is especially important when describing the few high-quality activities. Even the minor activities provide value and experiences. The interesting experiences from the minor activities can be incorporated whenever possible. Certain phrasing can help accurately express relatively minor activities while adding interest. For example, rudimentary Russian, novice Portuguese and etc can add interest in the application. It adds experiences that make your application unique. It may tie into your other experiences such as travel and experiences in a different country.

Interviews

The interviews for medical school are mostly multiple medical interviews in Canada. One-on-one or panel interviews tend to be used in the United States. If you get an interview, then you have already been selected from many other applicants. You should have added confidence in your application and interview. You have demonstrated that the medical school is interested in you. You have met the threshold for being accepted in the medical school. Generally, applicants at the interview stage, have relatively similar quality of application on paper. Effectively everyone would be qualified to be accepted into a medical school once they've made it to the interview stage. But there is another filtering process due to the limited number of seats. The interview is really to filter out the few candidates with red flags to suggest the lack of professionalism and ethics. Effectively nearly everyone could pass the interview. However, since there are limited number of seats, there a few things applicants can do to distinguish themselves and prepare for the interview. If you've made it to the interview, practicing and polishing the interview is generally the major thing that is left unless there a few things that are borderline in reaching the thresholds mention previously. There are other resources and books that provide guidance and instruction on medical school interviews and multiple mini interview for medical schools. Interview preparation is outside the scope of this book to go into detail. That being said, I will highlight the importance of practicing by recording yourself to improve delivery. The interview is also assessing for certain qualities outlined to be a physician. The qualities that can be assessed are collectively called the CanMEDS. The CanMEDS competencies are described below in the CanMEDS section. The qualities that could be assessed includes all the CanMEDS roles except for medical expert.

CanMEDS

The CanMEDS competencies are qualities identified to be important as a physician. CanMEDS are tested throughout medical school and residency. There are qualities that can be assessed prior to entering medical school that can come up during the interview. The CanMEDS competencies includes medical expert, leader, communicator, collaborator, scholar, professionalism, and health advocate. The medical expert role is obviously not tested in the applicant to medical school. Medical expertise is the purpose of medical school and residency. So the medical school applicant does not need to worry about that the role of medical expert. Leadership can be assessed with your prior extracurricular experiences. Prepare stories of you that demonstrate leadership such as organizing an event. Communicator can be tested by asking you for a time you dealt with conflict or difficult situation. Collaborator can be tested by your experience working with other groups, organizations, or team work. Professionalism can be assessed by asking for your behavior and response in an ethical scenario. Professionalism can also be tested by asking about your own experience in being professional and ethical. Scholar can include times when you had to teach or be involved in research. Collaboration in research can fulfill both research, collaborator and communicator roles.

MMI

The multiple mini interview (MMI) is designed to be fairer by having multiple interviewers assess the same candidate over several stations. Each station tests different aspects of the candidate. There are usually 6 to 12 stations. No single interviewer can bias the results excessively. This is supposed to be fairer compared to a single or panel interview. Single or panel interviews can result in one person with an undue amount of influence. The candidate will stand in front the door of a small room. The candidate has two minutes to read a question posted on the door. The candidate will hear a buzzer and enter the room. There is usually an interviewer sitting in the room. Sometimes the interviewer will have prepared standardized questions that they can ask the candidates. Often these are prompting questions to help the candidate address as many points regarding the question. The candidate is not penalized for having prompting questions. Some may have no prompting questions because they have already addressed all the relevant points. The candidate has a fixed amount of time in the room. The time in the room usually ranges from 5 to 10 minutes. The exact timing varies between the schools. If the candidate finishes the answer prior to the allotted time, they are asked to stay in the room until the allotted time has expired. Then the candidate will exit the room and move onto the next door. The process is repeated with the next question. The interviewers are often instructed not to give small talk, feedback and to remain as neutral as possible. This can be awkward especially, when the candidate has finished the answer and there is a fair bit of time left over. Finishing the question early doesn't necessarily mean the answer is too short or inadequate as long as all the relevant points have been addressed.

Results

After the interview, your job as the applicant is effectively done. There is nothing else you can do at this point but wait for the results. You should be proud to have gone this far in the application process. Many candidates have not gotten this far in the process. Celebrate, relax and do your best to enjoy the time after the interview. Try to not to think about the application. You've thought about the application long enough for the good part of the year already. It should be a relief to not have to think about it for once. The date for the release of results vary between the schools. In Canada, all the schools tend to release the results near the end of the school year. In the United States, the results tend to be released throughout the year. Most schools at this day and age release the results online or by email.

What do I do now that I got into medical school?

Congratulations on getting into medical school! It a dream come true that you have been striving for a long time. Take the time to enjoy the summer and celebrate prior to starting medical school. Spend some time preparing for the litany of paperwork and bureaucracy with starting medical school.

Getting into medical school feels like the end of a chapter. But it is also the beginning of a journey. During the first year of medical school, take some time to shadow different medical specialties to get an idea of what you want to specialize in residency. The earlier you get an idea, the better you can prepare. Some of the competitive specialties require preparation quite early in medical school.

Furthermore, early exposure allows you to get a better idea of how the medical system functions. Early exposure provides context when studying textbook information during the two years of Medicine.

What do I do if I don't get into medical school?

There are several options that will be reviewed sequentially. Should you try again? Consider medical schools abroad? Consider switching to another career? Consider graduate school?

Try again

If you have an interview, you are qualified to get into a medical school. It is a matter of time and refining your application. The important thing is not to be disheartened by this process. You are in good company. Many candidates require multiple rounds of applications before they got into medical school. The perseverance and psychological impact are probably the most difficult parts of this process. There are only so many components in the application that an applicant can be evaluated. If you're applying again, review the book again and focus on the aspects in the application that you can improve the most.

If you didn't get an interview, you can narrow down the areas of the application to work on. The potential areas to improve include all the components of the application discussed up to the interview. The good thing is that you have narrowed down the possible things you can do to work on to improve on your application. Hopefully, the things you need to work on are relatively easy to improve. If it is regarding grades, the best thing is to move forward by taking higher level courses. Alternatively, complete the remainder of the courses in your degree to bring up the average. Moving forward is better than trying to retake courses in an attempt to increase the average grade. If you're at the stage of nearing graduation, consider moving up to a graduate program. Taking another undergraduate degree or taking more courses to extend the degree is less effective than a graduate program. The strategy is outlined in more detail in the following sections labeled "Switch to an alternative career" and "Graduate School". Generally, moving forward provides more gains in value and improvement in your application than looking backwards. This is partly because the advancement is associated with more skills and experiences. For example, a graduate program is associated life experiences, new opportunities and references. Furthermore, psychologically, you will feel like you are advancing as opposed to feeling like you're stuck in a glut in your life. Spot fixing areas by taking or retaking courses to increase your grade may feel like a bandage approach. It is very difficult to take enough courses to bring up an average near the end of the degree. It is also difficult to do something drastically different compared to what you've been doing previously in the earlier courses. Grades also take less of an emphasis in the application process when you have a graduate degree. Grades are also less important after a certain age. After a certain age, usually 25 years old, some medical schools consider them to be mature applicants and have a lower weighting on grades. Review the mature applicant section of the application for each medical school if it is relevant to you. Remember, you only need your grade to meet the threshold. You don't need to spend excessive effort trying to get the highest mark. There are other parts of the application that needs to be taken care of as well.

If your grades and MCAT meet the threshold and you don't have a negative reference letter, then chances are you need to work on your extracurricular activities. Review the appropriate corresponding sections focusing on extracurricular activities. Perform more extracurricular activities, volunteering in medical and non-medical areas. If you already have significant medically related volunteering, then volunteering in non-medical areas that you have a significant interest can develop more experiences. More experiences and stories will help with making you a more interesting and unique candidate. Other than engaging in extracurricular activities, review if your presentation of the extracurricular activity gives enough justice for the work and experiences. Ensure the extracurricular activities are phrased as professional, concise and accurate as possible.

"Success is going from failure to failure without losing your enthusiasm"
Winston Churchill

Medical School Abroad

When considering the medical schools outside your country, the situation becomes more complex. Attending medical schools abroad is significantly more expensive with regards to the tuition and living expenses. Obtaining funding from banks is often more difficult. The credit limit for medical schools abroad is often less than for a local medical student. Government student loans are often not adequate. The culture, language, and health system can be very different abroad. It can take time to adjust when you're there. If you return to your own country, there can also be an adjustment coming back. If you go down the route of medical schools abroad, you need to be prepared for a longer and more difficult path. Be prepared for the possibility of never being able to return to your own country to practice. The benefit is that there is a very high chance you will get in. Most graduate and become physicians. The biggest sacrifice is the possibility that you won't be able to return to your own country to practice. However, the rules are becoming more welcoming for foreign medical graduates.

US MD Schools

The US medical school's MD program is the closest to Canadian medical schools. But they are still treated as foreign medical graduates. US medical graduates face a similarly difficult time in going into Canada. The advantage of US medical schools compared to other medical schools is the culture and training is more similar. The transition from US to Canada is generally smoother.

US DO Schools

The alternative pathway for medical schools includes the DO programs which has different emphasis. DO schools are generally easier to get in compared to the MD program. DO programs usually has a route that will allow you to practice as a physician.

Caribbean Medical Schools

The Caribbean schools mimic the US medical schools. But these schools are geographically located in the Caribbean for most of the training. The clinical rotations may be partly in the US. By passing the same exams as the US medical schools, the Caribbean medical graduates are generally able to integrate with the US medical graduates. The Caribbean schools are one of the easier medical schools to get in.

Australian Medical Schools

Australian medical schools are also easier to enter by favoring the international applicant for international spots. There are recruitment organizations for Australian medical schools that will facilitate the application process. The academic year start in January as opposed to September in North America. The academic year in Australia are offset so you may have a gap of a few months when returning into the North American medical education system for residency.

European Medical Schools

The European medical schools are like Australian schools in terms of admission difficulty. The European medical schools also have recruitment organizations. The main difference is a different geographic location and culture.

Switch to an alternative career

At this stage of life, you might want to consider if there are alternative careers and professions that you can achieve personal satisfaction and life goals. Weigh the positives and negatives of continuing to apply to medical school or switching to a different career. There is also the possibility of switching to another career while applying to medical school. Switching to an alternative career by attending graduate school while applying for medicine is further discussed in the graduate school section. The possibility of working while applying to medical school can be considered. Most schools will decrease the focus on past grades and look upon the applicant more favorably if they are older than 25 years old. If you are working or getting further education while reapplying, ensure you are doing things that will add value and strengthen your applications as opposed to reapplying with the same application year after year.

Graduate school

Graduate school is looked upon favorably in the medical school application. Graduate school provides higher education that distinguishes these candidates from other candidates. Some schools provide extra points in the ranking of their candidates for completing graduate school. Graduate school is beneficial in acquiring research and other transferable skills that can be used later in medical school, residency and in practice. Graduate school is sometimes completed by medical students and residents as part of their program. Completing a graduate program can be a method to get ahead start while still applying to get into medical school. The caveat is that if you decide to change to a different specialty, the graduate program may still be useful but may not be as useful if not as relevant. Some people go back to complete another undergraduate program or more undergraduate courses instead of graduate school. They may be attempting to increase their marks prior to reapplying to medical school. Although this is a viable option, this places a lot of emphasis on being able to get higher marks despite previous efforts. It can be difficult to bring up an average with a few additional courses, especially without taking many additional courses. Graduate school will provide added value to the application while de-emphasizing the grades. Furthermore, graduate school programs will be advancing your education for a potential profession or later in your medical profession when you get into medical school.

Many schools also de-emphasize the grades, add additional points, or view the applicant more favorable after a certain age, such as 25 years old. Maturity is a quality medical schools desire. Completing a graduate degree advances your credentials which can be combined with an older age to strengthen your application. At the same time, the focus on grades is minimized. People can be in graduate programs that provide an alternative profession if they don't get into medical school. The drawback with this method is that they may be entering and graduating from medical school at an older age. They may need to balance family planning with medical school.

Conclusion

Congratulations on finishing this book! You have a much better understanding of applying to medical school compared to other people who have not read this book. Review the sections in this book as you progress through the stages in the application process. Insights will take on a deeper meaning when you have personal experience in each of the stages. Using this book as a guide in your application will facilitate the application process. It may give you direction and confidence. Remember to keep life in perspective. Applying to medical school is a small part in the grander scheme of your entire life. Your career and profession will always be there waiting for you, but the relationships and other aspects of your life may not. Good luck!

Resources

Multiple Mini Interview for Medical School: The Essentials

By: Jordan Westley

The multiple mini interview can be made into a very complicated and stressful event. There are an infinite number of possible questions and scenarios. This book strives to simplify the multiple mini interview. Understand the interview from the interviewer's perspective. Learn an approach so you feel comfortable and confident in answering any question. Distillation of the MMI to the essence keeps it simple in your mind. This results in less chance of error during the stress of the interview. Practice with practice interview questions designed to simulate the real MMI. Knowledge and practice to help you answer interview questions with ease and confidence.

Multiple Mini Interview for Medical School: Practice Interview Series

By: Jordan Westley

Multiple Mini Interview for Medical School: Practice Interview Series Exam 1 by Jordan Westley

Multiple Mini Interview for Medical School: Practice Interview Series Exam 2 by Jordan Westley

Multiple Mini Interview for Medical School: Practice Interview Series Exam 3 by Jordan Westley

Practicing the multiple mini interview is essential to the success of the applicant. A full-length practice interview simulates the experience of the multiple mini interview. It prepares the applicant for the types of questions, stamina, and experience of the multiple medical interview. Review the marking sheets and discussions to gain insight from the interviewer's perspective. Practicing the interview experience helps prepare you to be confident and comfortable with the multiple mini interview.

www.ingramcontent.com/pod-product-compliance
Lightning Source LLC
Chambersburg PA
CBHW020415230426
43664CB00009B/1277